i

A Guide for Young Entrepreneurs

Adrian Clark

2016 Winner

Foreword
by Errol Spence, Jr.

Before I stepped into the ring for my first professional boxing match, I trained as an amateur for several years to become the No. 1 ranked boxer in the world going into the Olympics. In that time, the way amateur boxing was structured, I never knew who I'd be fighting next.

There was little to no time to analyze my opponent's strengths and weaknesses, to plot my own strategy around them. So, like any other athlete, I had to rely on the principles I learned in training. Those principles worked for me no matter who else was in the ring. That's a winning strategy.

My friend, entrepreneur Adrian Clark, works much the same way, as a boxing manager. In all the time I've known him, he's always been ready, or at least he's never been "not ready," for whatever was about to come his way.

Now he's done everyone who reads this book a huge favor by breaking his winning strategy down into bite-size lessons that anyone can absorb. That's Adrian's style, and it's the main lesson of his book: You don't know what's coming next, so ground yourself in proven principles from the beginning of your career as an entrepreneur.

Even more helpful is that Adrian doesn't simply repeat the old but true advice, "You are what you think." He answers the next question, "What should I think?"

Adrian's a disciplined and calculated guy. You'll see that for yourself here, as he shares exactly what you will need to discipline yourself and plot your future as an entrepreneur.

When I'm in the ring, I am totally comfortable and sure of victory because of my preparation in training camp. Adrian provides you proper preparation with this guide. So when you're in the ring of life, you can be just as comfortable and confident as I am.

Only a few people can become world-class athletes. But many, many more can find success in business, whether it's a sports-related enterprise or not.

Let Adrian's book be your map through the minefield of entrepreneurship. He knows where the mines are. He's stepped on a few!

About i

i began my entrepreneurial journey at age 23, fresh out of college. i set myself up with a unique opportunity and took full advantage. i've put up my own money for everything to do with AC Sports Management, LLC. i never had an investor. There was no consistent mentor and no such thing as a partner. i'd be lying if i said i got here by myself, but i'd also be downplaying myself if i failed to say, "i built my name, my company, and my reputation with little to no assistance."

Now, looking back on my six years as an entrepreneur, i decided to write this guide for young entrepreneurs to assist young men and women who are looking to create and build off of their name and passions. In hindsight, i never knew how long six years was until i thought about the experiences, the opportunities, and the people that i've met, dealt with, and experienced.

Growing up in the inner city of Dallas, Texas, we thought sports was the way out—football or basketball, your choice. Of course, college was discussed but for some of us, it was only thought of from a student-athlete standpoint. i mean, who goes to school, just to learn … right?

i honestly never learned about entrepreneurship. It was not a subject in school. None of my friends or family were entrepreneurs; so naturally i paid no mind to the word or its meaning.

The two things that were instilled in me (and a lot of the kids from the inner city) were "sports" and "job." But i knew i didn't want someone telling me what to do. i didn't want to call someone else "boss" when, all my life, i looked at myself to be just that: the boss.

i stand behind every chapter in this book because it all happened to me along my journey.

For anyone looking to follow my example, know that the early stages and transitions will be extremely tough. i took a leap of faith on myself and it paid off, but it took so many losses to get there. Although other entrepreneurial guides may exist, this is not one that is guiding you on how to build a brand and get richer than Richie. i wrote this in hopes that you sidestep the mistakes i made on my journey and prepare for what lies ahead better than i did.

i don't do it often, but occasionally i'll look back down the path and revisit where i came from, in my mind. The year 2013 is one i dread to revisit but it's the year that i honestly earned my stripes as an entrepreneur. For starters, i breached a contract on an investment that i knew was going to fail! i went against my greater judgment and thought about the money that was to come.... Long story short, i settled out of court and lost all i had saved plus more. i had just bought a luxury townhouse and sports car. i panicked and got a job at Gold's Gym as a personal trainer.

On top of getting sued and working at Gold's, i made one of the dumbest decisions of my life regarding the money to pay for the settlement. It all blew up in my face before i could fix it. To top it all off, one of my best friends died unexpectedly at home.

At my lowest point in life (thus far) i decided that giving up wouldn't help anything. i quit Gold's (after five days), turned the garage of my luxury townhouse into a boxing gym, and made flat money teaching people how to box. Along with that, i became all-in focused on my company and worked night and day texting, calling, emailing anyone in the boxing industry to get my guy a chance to fight. Got the fight, got the win, negotiated a world-title fight that earned not only my client his biggest payday, but one for me also. The year 2014 was my best financially as an entrepreneur. But 2013 was my worst year as an entrepreneur, all around.

Notice the turnaround? i have to strongly reiterate, the smartest thing i have ever done as an entrepreneur was NEVER GIVE UP! i've had a six-figure deal agreed to and shaken on, only to receive a 14-page text from the potential partner pulling out of the deal. i've had people seek me out, tell me they were going to deal with me, and promise multi-million-dollar backing, but ultimately, they never dealt with me. i've had people try to use me to their benefit. In return, they sold me a dream of investing in my company. Once their attempt to use me was unsuccessful, they moved on … with their investment. i tell you, i've seen all of what the early stages can bring and i've faced them all head-on!

As you see, i'm still here, moving forward amicably, creating and building my brand, reminding myself of what i started saying in college: "Do what you have to do now, so you can do what you want to do later!" i have a very limited number of friends nowadays. i'd rather work more than play and i surround myself with people who make me better and live above society's tent. It is the sacrifice i make for greatness; you, too will have to make some sacrifices.

Be inspired and motivated by this guide! It will not be an easy journey, but follow the chapters and know the sky is NOT the limit. (Think about it; Neil Armstrong would agree!) If i can make it with no investor, partner, or mentor, then you, too, can make it just as far as i have.

On completion of this guide, you will have knowledge of things that i had no clue of starting out as an entrepreneur. Don't ever forget your "why" and don't ever forget "i."

(Why "i"? Because it takes growth, experience and credibility to be an upper-case i. The level of entrepreneurs i'm writing toward are regarded as the lower-case i, looking to gain the growth, experience and credibility to be looked at as an upper-case I. That's the reason for the lower case i throughout this book.

And the title came from my mother telling me, "i knew when i had you that your ass was going to be selfish. Your favorite word is "i." This book is like an autobiography and motivational guide/manual wrapped into one: What better title than "i"?)

Acknowledgements

Although i was only in the 4th grade, i was drawn to this woman in a way that i can't totally put into words; i just knew that i loved her. i excelled in her class because i wanted to impress her every chance i got. My incredible progress showed her genius because she used my infatuation with her against me. She knew she could put me on the spot to volunteer or answer a question correctly, because she knew i wanted her praise. Now that i think about it, she used me emotionally and took advantage of me academically. Damn. She was, and still is, an amazing educator. To the great **Mignon Hansford**: i wouldn't have the ability to do this if it were not for you.

By age 9, i knew how to sit down with an adult and have a full conversation, intelligently. That's the only way i could hang out with **Dr. James Reed** in his office. i had to speak and conduct myself

like an adult, but i was just a kid. He was a
0-nonsense type of guy, but also a leader
in every sense of the word. You could see
him in commercials, magazines, books,
and newspapers. He was the first black
man i saw in a position of influence
besides my dad. i wanted that
recognition. i wanted that fame. i wanted
to be viewed like "Doc" was viewed. "If
it's meant to be, it's up to me." i used to
hate having to recite that every morning
at school. i didn't know what it meant,
then. But as an adult, i know why Dr. Reed
used to make us say it every day. Thanks
for the example of greatness, old man.

In 2004, i was senior class president and a
sports writer for the school newspaper.
One day i got into an argument with my
journalism instructor about adulthood.
She told me, "One day, you are going to
have a boss to answer to." At that point in
life, i'd never had a job, but i knew one
thing as a 16-year-old with a smart-ass
mouth; i never wanted a "boss." i rudely

expressed that i would never have a boss (among other things) and from there i was sent to in-house suspension. i'm pretty sure i was the ONLY class president in high-school history to be sent to in-house suspension. Thank you, **Margie Luck**, for challenging me and sending me to school jail.

Two weeks after i graduated from college, the 34th pick in the 2005 NBA draft and my childhood friend allowed me to move in with him and be a part of his professional basketball career. The history that he, Bleek, and i made in Salt Lake City will be impossible to repeat. There is no way i can speak on the beginning of my career and not mention how he made things easier for me to be who i am today. i still remember, as a kid, getting ready for bed at night but he was still outside with that damn basketball getting better when he could have been in bed, too. From childhood to adulthood, from the amazing times we had to the horrible times we endured: Thank you, **CJ Miles**.

To this day, i still wonder, "What the hell were you thinking?" when deciding to hire me. i had no previous knowledge of the business. i had zero connections and not to mention i was 24 years old (six months removed from college). Although the odds were against us, we overly succeeded and innovated the relationship between Boxer and Manager. We made it to a world title and got to travel the world to do what we love. JB, you are one of my best friends and will always be. To AC Sports Management, LLC's very first client, **Jerry "The Corpus Christi Kid" Belmontes**, thank you.

i have been an entrepreneur for going on six years now: no investor; no mentor; no partner. Just a dollar and a dream. Besides my dad, this amazing, family-first man was the only person to occasionally add to my dollar to see my dream come

to fruition. He has been an amazing
influence on me and he will go down in
history as one of the most generous Texas
A&M University alumni. You are the man,
Mr. Mac, always have been, always will
be. Thank you for always telling me,
"Good always wins in the end."

Although he is often times "unplugged
from the matrix," i have the luxury of
saying that i have the best stylist in the
city. Along with saying that, i can also
attribute my reasoning for being an
entrepreneur to **Germaine Byrd**.
i remember as a kid going to Ronny J's
with my dad to get a haircut. Abdul was
the man at that time; he owned the shop
but "G" (Germaine) was young and cool;
i always went to him. Before i knew it,
i was at "Studio Essence." G owned this
shop and designed it to fit himself. i never
understood how he did it ... until now. G
was the first true entrepreneur i ever
encountered. i learned a great deal from

him, not realizing at the time that i was learning a great deal from him!

To my lifetime investors, my mom and pops, **Anthony & Loriette Clark**

i am not sure what you guys were doing while you were conceiving me but it must have been some next-level, unconventional, untraditional stuff, because your youngest son is for sure all of those things. As a little boy, i remember Dad waking up while it was still dark out to go put in work so we could have the shoes and clothes we wanted. i remember mom was always so stern and strict! She spoke so fast and aggressively also, very intimidating at times. Now as an adult when i look at them, i see exactly why i am the entrepreneur that i am today. My personality and intangibles that i inherited from them would not allow me to do anything else. The way they both raised my older brother Brandon and me forced greatness out of us. i have the perfect combination of traits from them both. Although i am very quiet and observant like dad, i can talk people's ear off and be very bossy like my mama. The incredible work ethic i have is from my father. My ability to speak very well and aggressively to get my point across is from my mother. i know sometimes they wonder what the hell i'm doing as an entrepreneur. The only answer i have for them is: i'm doing what they conceived, raised, and pushed me to be. i promised Brandon that i would never give up on something i loved ever again. In his death, i honor my promise and every time i think about him not being here i go harder for all of us. i love you both more than anything else in this universe.

Adrian Clark

Contents

i

Introduction

The ninth letter in the alphabet refers to YOU! Own it, learn to love it, and believe in that letter (i) more than you believe in anything else on planet Earth.

As an entrepreneur in America, you will endure many hardships; no two struggles are exactly the same. Embrace your struggles just as tightly as you cling on to your successes. Understand that it is YOU (i) that will either guide your ship to its destination or wreck it in the harbor.

In order to understand "i," you must understand who you are, what you are about, and where you want to go. Learning on the fly is cool in business, but learning on the fly in regards to self— while trying to learn on the fly as an entrepreneur—is a recipe for destruction. Learn who you are first.

"i" is a guide for young entrepreneurs that presents pointers in the areas of decision-making, sacrifice, risk, strategic planning, and other entrepreneurial principles.

The philosophy of "i" is a framework that only you should be able to map out. The philosophy of "i" is presented here in short, concise statements. These proverbial statements are designed to better prepare you mentally for your entrepreneurial journey.

Use this guide and strive ultimately to be successful on your entrepreneurial journey, but read this guide with thoughts of longevity and preparation. Everyone's "success" level and definition will be different. Your experiences as an entrepreneur will provide you the brushes to paint your canvas of success once your journey is complete. Paint your own masterpiece! Do not trace that of another man's success and look to make it yours.

Once you've completed and closed this book, you will know more about the entrepreneurial grind than you know at this exact moment. Your journey begins here....

1

Passion

=

Paycheck

---

*Get paid in the process
of perfecting your
passion!*

We were each given a gift at birth. You'll
often find that the gift you possess comes
naturally. Think about a person you know
who can draw anything on request: they
didn't attend art school or practice for
countless hours; they just know how to

illustrate anything, perfectly. Most times, that gift or talent becomes a passion for that individual, who eventually begins to devise a formula on how to turn that passion into a paycheck.

Before marketing your talents, ask yourself a few questions:

- Is my passion in demand?
- Is there longevity in my passion?
- If my passion belonged to someone else, would i buy what they were selling?

If you answered "yes" to any of those questions, then moving forward will be easier for you as an entrepreneur.

Getting started, target your friends, friends of friends, family, and other associates. If they are really supporters they will either buy your service or market it to others. From there, market yourself on the social networks and show your passion to possible consumers, strangers,

and lovers of your particular passion.
Build a fan base. Build a brand.

Don't sell yourself or your passion short.
Get paid in the process of perfecting your
passion! With that being said, do not fall
in love with the paycheck over your
passion! If you are good at what you do
and you have the marketing behind it, the
money will come. Stay true to yourself
and stay true to your passion.

2

Who Knows You?

In a room full of ordinary, "different" is remembered.

---

it's not "what you know." Hell, it's not even "who you know."

It's actually "who knows you"! Understand that your "network" is indeed your "net worth" but it doesn't amount to anything substantial if the individuals you are reaching out to can't identify with who you are, or what it is you do.

People do not have to know your life's story to know you. Your name being brought up in a positive light by a third party can be more valuable than one person knowing your life story. How will they remember you? What will stand out about you?

Often times, people will back you solely because of YOU! Your name and reputation is essentially all you have as entrepreneur (and in life).

Learn different icebreaker and initiation tactics to meet people. Sometimes a joke or a false sense of nostalgia can leave a lasting impression on someone to remember you at face- or voice-value.

If you notice someone wearing a distinctive accessory, such as a ring, or scarf, or even a stylish pair of shoes, make a complimentary mention of it. People wear such things to get attention, and they appreciate when it's noticed. Elaborate on the item and maybe even say you have one similar to it. At that point, you guys have something to connect on. From there, allow them to go into detail about what you now have in common. Sometimes relation solidifies recognition, which forces remembrance later on for people.

Be not afraid to be different. In a room full of ordinary, "different" is remembered.

The most important thing is that you uphold both your name and rep to the highest standards. You do that, and people will remember your name and respect your reputation.

3

Shut Up and Listen

---

*Most people's favorite
topic is themselves.*

If it's true that you have to learn to follow
before you can effectively lead, then you
should really learn to listen effectively
before you speak. Older, seasoned
entrepreneurs that have survived the
struggle to become successful don't want
to hear about your guts and glory. In fact,
they want you to sit and listen to their
glory stories and if you dare to have any
questions, they better be toward what
you've been hearing in their story!

If what goes around comes around, then listen to those who have been around when you come around! Speak only when cued or questioned; look to deflect as many questions as possible back at your elder counterpart. Make them feel that you are indeed listening and care (even if you don't). That time you spent listening and taking notes can result in learning things you didn't know beforehand, but most importantly, it buys you his/her ear when you need to ask for a favor one day.

Most people's favorite topic is themselves. Use that to your advantage and ask your counterpart if you can interview them. At least with interviewing, you can control the direction of the conversation. Sure, "shut up and listen" is the basis, but no one wants to listen to a lecture. Be sure to ask open-ended (not yes-or-no) questions and do your due diligence!

4

Move in Silence

---

*Don't tell friends,
family, spouse, or
followers what's in the
works.*

No one can take anything of value from
you. For that to occur, you would have to
give it away by putting yourself in a
position for something to be taken from
you.

No one can take your ideas and make
them work as you would have unless you
allow them to. Your ideas are in your
head. Even if someone cuts your head off

and takes it, they just have your head; still not your ideas. The ONLY other way someone can get inside your head is for you to tell them what is in there.

Keep inside what you know and have a "non-disclosure agreement" handy if you choose to let someone in on what you have brewing. Think of a mad scientist: He didn't label himself "mad"; it was actually the people who couldn't see what he was working on behind the laboratory doors that labeled him that. Scientists are secretive and mum, but only while projects are being worked on. After the product is finished, you can't shut them up on what they have done and what they have been doing!

Be a "mad entrepreneur," and don't tell friends, family, spouse, or followers what's in the works. They'll expect it to happen by tomorrow! And if it doesn't happen, you will be faced with questions that you probably would not want to answer anyway, because you are still pissed that your idea fell through. Move, in total silence and look to bring the noise once everything is complete.

5

Surrounded By

Surround yourself with those who will keep you working for more.

Along your journey you'll eventually see "who is who" and "what is what" in regard to the people that make up your circle. It is imperative that you see people for who they are showing you they are, and not who you knew them to be from the past. Don't be afraid to let people go … for now.

Think of it as if you are the sun. You are surrounded by planets that are "near" to you. We all know the sun feeds energy to the planets; it becomes destructive, though, if the planets were to fail in their orbit. Without distance and motion, the planets would get pulled into the sun and destroyed.

It's the same with people: If the people close to you don't move around (orbit) from time to time, then the relationships are burned by way of the sun (you).

Surround yourself with:

- people who would rather work than play a majority of the time
- entrepreneurs who have taken the same sacrifice as you; they somewhat understand your "why" (defined in *Enjoy the Process*)
- positive energy and individuals who will "keep it real" with you despite who you are or what you've done.

Sometimes that one friend who has no filter is the best person to be around because he/she won't pull punches when it comes to you and what you are doing.

Although you are not in direct competition with the people who make up your circle, silently treat it as such. Watch the people that are surrounding you and observe their accomplishments.

If you are surrounded by people who aren't making moves and you are in competition with yourself, complacency will find its way into your career. Surround yourself with those who will keep you working for more. When they make strides, put pressure on yourself to make a move also. Do not let them go off and leave you sitting still. Compete!

6

Handle With Care

---

*We can't control what
people say but we can
control how we treat
them.*

Understand that everyone is an
opportunity. As entrepreneurs, we are
the walking billboard. We are what "our"
brand stands for. We NEED people! So
with that being said, handle people you
meet carefully. You never know who you
could be speaking with or in front of!

Once the ice is broken, keep the
relationship friendly but business-

professional. Ask questions and stay current with people. Keep 'em talking, even if it's about themselves. (AGAIN, people love to do that!)

In this day and age, the Internet tells everything. When speaking about yourself, be honest, but not too revealing. Don't embellish your situation, and be leery of people who embellish theirs. Embellishment sells books, not people, but even in a situation where someone added to their legend, don't think them to be, or treat them as, a liar; they still may be beneficial to you.

We can't control what people say but we can control how we treat them to curb what they will say to others. Network with the mindset that, "This person may know this person; and that person knows this person."

Also, be the initiator! Don't wait for them to reach out; be the first one to text, email, or call. You are building the network! On bad days when you completely don't want to be bothered, you have to put on your "all people are welcomed" mask and save the tantrum for behind closed doors. You belong to the people when you're outside, so fake it until you make it … home.

7

Plan, Strategically

Don't look to "cross that bridge when you get there."

The future is not guaranteed, but while you're taking care of today, prepare for tomorrow.

Anyone without a plan will go round and round before ever going straight. You have to know what you want; otherwise you will continuously deal with bullshit that won't get you what you want.

Even planning strategically calls for you to know the consequences of your acts. Just because it was thought out perfectly doesn't mean snags won't occur. Based on your planned calculations, what "snags" possibly could occur? What is your move if snags occur? What is the consequence of this snag? This way of planning keeps you disciplined and on your toes. It also keeps you grounded and sticking to the ultimate plan.

Don't look to "cross that bridge when you get there." You know troubled waters are coming; know what you are going to do before you get there. Stick to your plan! Don't deviate from something you strategically planned months or years beforehand! Timing is everything! So, aside from minor adjustments, trust in your plan and execute as mapped out in the blueprint.

8

Bearded Sacrifice

---

*Things you sacrificed
will resurface, possibly
in better form.*

What will you sacrifice to be the best?
Since you have chosen the life of an
entrepreneur, you clearly are willing to
sacrifice your livelihood ... but what else?

You cannot expect to be successful at
anything without sacrifice. You have to
understand that sacrifice is essential as an
entrepreneur.

Sacrifice is like a thief, robbing you at gunpoint: "What else you got? What else do you have to give up, to live?"

Will you sacrifice the next two years of your life for the next 50 years? Saying yes sounds good but "doing" yes looks even better.

There is a price to success as an entrepreneur. Your sacrifice will naturally take you away from people, places, and things not on a similar path as you. Don't fret about things that you selected to sacrifice; in case you haven't noticed, history often repeats itself! Things you sacrificed will resurface, possibly in better form.

Quick side-note story about an entrepreneur who made a great sacrifice: There was a man that had been growing his beard for years. He loved his beard damn near more than he loved people. He combed, conditioned, washed and shampooed his beard every day. It was one of his prized possessions.

One day, the man was sitting in his office and he looked at his desk, which was piled with paperwork, projects, and proposals he had been dragging his feet on, but he needed to finish them. He left his office, went to his barber and told him to cut off his beard. The barber pleaded with him not to, but the man shook his head and said, "cut it." People who knew the man all wanted to know why, but the man never revealed why he cut his beard.

Over time, the man's beard began to grow back and people recognized the growth, yet continued to ask why he cut it; the man never revealed why. Months later at the barber shop, the man's stylist asked while trimming his beautiful, thick beard, "Why did you go through all of that; cutting your beard for no reason, only to grow it back? That didn't make any sense." The man chuckled and told his stylist to meet him at his office after the haircut.

The stylist went by the office while the man sat behind his desk running his fingers through his beard. "This is why i cut my beard," the man said. The stylist looked around the office, which was spotless, and said, "i don't get it, this office is why you cut your beard? There is nothing here to explain your actions. Look at your desk; nothing is on it. No paperwork, projects or proposals! Cut the crap and tell me why you cut it!" The man laughed and said, "Sacrifice."

Just in case you missed it (shame on you if you did): The man got behind on work and decided to challenge himself to finish all of the tasks at hand. He sacrificed his beard. If he met or completed work before or on the set deadlines, then he did not cut the beard, giving it room to grow. If he failed to meet deadlines or fell back into procrastinating, then he had to cut the growth. The more you cut or shave your hair follicles, the less of a chance that the hair grows back at all. So if the man did not do what he was supposed to do, then not only would he

lose his beard but he would lose his deals
also.

9

Home Run Risk

*If you are worried
about going broke,
you'll never get rich.*

Let's be frank: You'll never get rich or be independent working for someone else unless you own a piece of the company.

In the entrepreneurial life, you are going to strike out countless times. The more you are up to bat, the more pitches you experience, the better the adjustments you'll make to eventually hit a homer! It only takes one home run to get on the scoreboard.

You can get rich working for yourself. You can also go broke working for yourself. But if you are worried about going broke, you'll never get rich.

Step up to the plate and swing for the fences. As an entrepreneur, just "getting on base" doesn't do much when you are the only batter available.

If you intend to get rich, you're going to have to take chances. In taking chances, you're going to go broke from time to time, but remember this: there is a huge difference between "going" broke and "being" broke. As long as you are plotting, scheming, strategizing, and moving, you will never be "broke." The moment you give up and stop moving, you'll be broke as a joke—and no one finds that funny.

Hitting a home run is not just brute strength. It takes precision, accuracy, timing, and focus also. The same attributes are required for making lots of money as an entrepreneur. You will not hit a home run holding the bat trying not to strike out. It may take a couple times at the plate but once you get that first homer ... *the crowd goes wild!*

10

Proposition, Don't Ask

Pride only hurts you as an entrepreneur; it never helps.

If you need investment to realize your plan, "asking" a possible investor for $100,000 will more than likely get you a swift, yet stern, NO. "Propositioning" a possible investor for $100,000 with a business plan and collateral may get you what you were looking for. Either way, proposition them if you need help; don't just "ask." (No, it is not the same thing).

A huge part of the propositioning phase is a well-drawn-up business plan. It is important that you get with people who have experience drawing up and reading business plans and contracts. Without a strong and thorough business plan, you are "asking" for start-up funds ... it is very far from a proposition. You have to show investors what you want to do; how you are going to do it; and most importantly, how much money are you bringing them back and how long it's going to take.

Most entrepreneurs don't have the capital to fully maximize their ideas. Be a smart self-starter. If given the opportunity, champ at the bit to proposition investors on why to invest in YOU and your company.

Don't be a fool in regards to entrepreneurial business. The prideful entrepreneur will waste years trying to "take the man route." (That's just pride, messing with you). Pride ... FORGET PRIDE! Pride only hurts you as an entrepreneur; it never helps.

Remember, you are selling yourself, not a bunch of figures and words on a PowerPoint. Be prepared to present the figures but don't lean on them to close the deal. If you have a history of success, your future says the same. There's good reason why someone who sells a successful business has to sign a "non compete" agreement with the buyer. They're what made the success happen! Sell yourself, your idea, and your past. Sell YOU!

11

Keep Calm

It is important that you always take the high road.

Always keep calm and be confident in your decisions. Always be at peace with yourself even when things are not right at the moment. Trust: With time and perseverance, things will be right again. Be patient.

Trust but verify, and always observe before making a move. You have to move cautiously in business but you also need to be daring. Ensure that the balance is good or it could turn into you being too cautious and missing opportunities. Or you can be too daring and mess everything up. Don't get in a hurry! This race is a marathon, not a sprint! Patience and timing are key, so take your time.

Keep calm when handling people. As we touched on in *Handle With Care*, there will be countless times in your journey when people are going to be mean, short, or dismissive toward you, especially in the beginning when you're a nobody! It is important that you always take the high road; be courteous, kind, and calm. No need to burn bridges when you are laying the foundation!

Keep that same humility once you make it. Don't build a brand being known as the "calm and collected guy to know," then make it to the mountaintop and turn into an asshole. Practice meditation and other forms of deep thinking to calm the mind and body. In any setting, remain as cool as the other side of the pillow.

12

Successful Failures

---

*It is our failures that
shape us, not our
successes.*

Your level of success will depend on your
ability to handle and overcome your
failures. Falling short of a goal or being
told NO sucks at that point in time. NO is
not the end of all ends as long as you
believe in your idea and understand what
persistence can get you. You'll appreciate
the NOs you received once you are told
"YES."

Often times it takes pain to make the brain a little smarter. That same pain is a feeling most don't want to feel over and over again, so you tend to work harder yet smarter in the aftermath of the rejected attempt.

Understand, it is our failures that shape us ... not our successes. The feeling of success is amazing only if you've experienced failure. Imagine never experiencing what it feels like to fail; would you even feel "successful"? The appreciation of both success and failure will take you far as an entrepreneur.

It is very important not to shut down if and when you do fail. Don't be afraid of the word "failure"; it actually means "success." Understand and embrace that you are going to fall short ... more than once. When you do fall, find out why, learn what you did incorrectly, and be better from it.

13

Thinking Things

If you plant positive thoughts, then your mind will grow positive thoughts.

If you plan to make a killing as an entrepreneur, the murder has to be premeditated. Think everything through before moving forward; every step has to be calculated. Thinking things through allows you to be prepared and have a backup plan, just in case.

Think for yourself. Seeking advice is one thing, but totally adopting another's thought process in regard to your idea is foolish.

Tread softly and heighten your awareness. You've heard the saying, "Think before you speak"? Please exercise this option often. This prevents you from talking out of your ass and saying something that was ill-thought-of. Also remember, you become what you think about. ("A man is what he thinks about all day long." —Ralph Waldo Emerson)

Think of your mind as a farm or garden. Be very aware what you plant in your mind! Your mind, very much like a farm or garden, does not care what you plant in it. If you plant negative thoughts, then your mind will grow negative thoughts which, more than likely, will produce negative results. If you plant positive thoughts, then your mind will grow positive thoughts, which will, more than likely, produce positive results.

As an entrepreneur, you will eventually train yourself to trick your mind to "know" everything will be fine—that $27.50 in your bank account is actually $2700.50; the bank is just holding the other zeroes for a later date.

Especially in the beginning stages of entrepreneurship, the process is so up-and-down that you have to think 90 percent positive and 10 percent negative. The 90 percent is similar to Batman and Robin being tied up with all the goons around them and it looks like for sure doom and there's only five minutes left in the show. Miraculously, Batman pushes a button on his belt, it cuts the chains off him and Robin, and they subdue the goons and save the day.

Regardless of how grim the situation, you have to possess that 90 percent and believe anything is possible as long as you're in control. That 10 percent negative is like you falling asleep in class and having a dream that you failed the semester, couldn't graduate, and had to start working in Corporate America.

Exactly: Get your ass up and get to work. That 10 percent is about scaring yourself to success. Remember, you are working for your life because you are terrified of a day job. Save the day! Think prosperous things that will guide your career further! Only think in negative terms to rattle yourself into getting things done.

14

Stupid Decisions

---

*You know when
something is not, or
does not, feel right.*

Refrain from making dumbass decisions
that will be detrimental to your career, let
alone your life. While on your
entrepreneurial journey, you are going to
be responsible for making huge decisions
every day. Sometimes those decisions will
include the livelihood of others. Learn and
understand the consequences of your
acts!

Going against "what you know" is one of the dumbest decisions you could make as an entrepreneur. Stupid decisions could leave you broke and outside of the entrepreneurial life. It is your company; go with your gut feeling based on what you know is right! You know when something is not, or does not feel right. Follow that feeling; don't be stupid.

Stupid Decisions:

- Doing anything that could land you in prison.
- Doing anything that will result in sudden death of yourself or others.
- Totally following others' advice or opinions (not developing your own).
- Intentionally wasting YOUR time.
- Burning bridges.
- Ruining your OWN name/reputation.
- Not developing a strong work ethic.

- Not having a premeditated plan.
- Having people that are detrimental to your growth surrounding you.
- Giving up.

15

Success Is a Fickle Mistress

For now, building your business is your full-time job.

Love is a very finicky character. If you had to choose one—love life or entrepreneur life—which do you go with? Do you need love or success more? Be advised that your commitment to your company could conflict with your commitment to the person you love. It is imperative that your partner understand your grind, struggle, and hustle damn near more than you do.

The more they understand and support, the better for you both.

Try to balance your love life and livelihood but take heed of the extreme challenges intimate relationships bring forth. As you should know, you can't make anyone truly happy until you make yourself happy first. You have to put "self" first in the early stages.

If you have ever flown on a plane, you know that flight attendants tell you before the plane takes off: "If there is a drop in cabin pressure, oxygen mask will drop from the bin above. PUT YOUR MASK ON FIRST, then proceed to help others." There will come a time when you can put your spouse before your work because things are where you want them to be. Right now is not that time.

For now, building your business is your full-time job! Your relationship will be the volunteer work you do on the side because you love it and have developed a passion for it. The moment the

relationship begins to feel like job #2—
you know, the job you hate but you are
doing it for a little extra money to make
ends meet—at that point you need to
RUN FOR YOUR LIFE! (Seriously, if the
person you are with cannot or does not
support what you have going on.) The
focus you are going to need to get things
done needs not to be tampered with or
altered, especially by someone that is not
YOU.

16

Value Your Vision More than the Money

---

*As often as possible,
remind yourself why
you are doing this.*

We have all heard the saying, "Don't forget where you came from." There is a similar saying in our world: "Don't forget why you chose to become an entrepreneur." Money never sleeps and can be made every day in many different ways. Entrepreneurship is hardly about the money because the money will never equal your name, your reputation ... your vision.

Trust and believe you will be blinded by the money often, especially when times get rough. You have to stay true to your vision. If it's only about the money, then go collect salary on someone else's watch. The entrepreneurial life is about creating a legacy and being remembered for starting something!

Have you ever been to a funeral and they talk about how much money the individual died with? You can be a multi-millionaire but no one will remember your name or legacy if you aren't leaving anything behind but the money.

As often as possible, remind yourself why you are doing this. Despite the naysayers and negativity around you, know why you are doing this and believe in your "why." Regardless of the hard times and lack of money, trust in your work ethic and continue to create.

Do this for your vision. Do this for your last name. Do this for your legacy. Chase the vision, not the money.

17

Patience, Young Grasshopper

Some deals can take months to finish; other deals can take longer.

Everything takes time ... especially as an entrepreneur! You'll find the moment you begin to rush things or force work, it won't come out right. You have to strike when the iron is hot, but even that iron takes time to heat up.

Really exercise patience when closing deals. Be careful not to rush your counterpart or seemingly force them into dealing with you. A business deal has to be treated like meeting someone special. You don't ask them to marry you as soon as you meet them, right? You take your time and wait for certain things to open up.

The same rules apply in business: Some deals can take months to finish; other deals can take longer. It is a stressful process if you aren't occupying your time in multiple ways. The more you have going on, the better your patience will be. Your mind and time won't be centered on this one deal, and that's important for sanity.

Becoming insanely impatient means you're either too focused on this one deal or that you don't have any other distraction in business ... or in life, for that matter.

It is possible that you can practice and gain patience in your everyday life outside of business. If you have pets, kids, a spouse, or unruly family members, you can practice on heightening your patience with handling situations in regards to your loved ones differently—or with better patience and understanding. As an entrepreneur, you are going to need patience … a lot of it.

18

Don't Forget to Play

Sometimes we have to forget work and be like everyone else.

All work and no play is ... well, hell, it's boring! Think of a guy who ONLY focuses on work and nothing else: No social life, very few friends, no experiences ... just work. Sure, he has a six-figure salary and works 80 hours a week for a Fortune 500 company, but let's be honest: This guy is just a well-paid zombie!

As entrepreneurs, we work 80 hours a week for ourselves so we don't have to work 80 hours a week for someone else!

Think of the best experiences of your young life: Are any of them work-related? HELL, NO! Don't forget to let your hair down and enjoy life itself!

In the entrepreneurial life, sometimes we have to forget work and be like everyone else for a very short period of time. Going out with school chums or friends to have one hell of a time actually sharpens your sword and refreshes your mind from business.

Don't take work so seriously that you lose yourself and the great experiences that are supposed to make up your life. At least twice a month (unless you have a huge project coming up) take a road trip, fly out of town, or throw a party with some friends. Play can give you ideas that you never would have thought of working in closed chambers.

Allow this segment to be a part of your balance as an entrepreneur. You know what you are working toward, and having a little fun will not warp your path and lead you astray. Remember, money and stature won't mean much without the utterly amazing experiences.

19

Everyone Else

---

*Why waste time
looking around at
others who are not in
the likes of you?*

Looking around at everyone else only
prolongs the process of success, and at
other times gives you a false sense of how
you should be as an entrepreneur.

As an entrepreneur, you are not like them
and they are not like you, whatsoever. As
much as the social networks are
extremely beneficial to entrepreneurship
these days, they are also detrimental to

the minds of people who are looking too hard at others. Magazine profiles, Facebook posts, websites, etc., only show you everyone else's final product. You live every day working on your first and second draft.

i repeat: "You're an entrepreneur." You do not have set work hours/schedule like everyone else. You do not have benefits like everyone else. You are not safe with weekly, bi-weekly, or monthly money like everyone else. You do not have paid time off or sick days like everyone else.

We can contrast entrepreneurship and Corporate America for days but ask yourself this question; "Why waste time looking around at others who are not in the likes of you?"

Focus on yourself and your business. Do not look to convince everyone else that they need to become entrepreneurs. Just as you have your "why" as an entrepreneur, they possess their "why" as a patron in Corporate America.

It is not our place to judge or recruit, for that matter. Be aware of this, though: There will be numerous times that "everyone else" will vent to you about how they are tired of working for someone else. They will then speak about their passions and what they "should" be doing. This often times is a ploy for them to have you hype them up on crossing over to our side.

Tread softly when doing so. Arrange one meeting with this individual to counsel them on the entrepreneurial life. Be blunt and brutal in your approach of educating them. Provide them with various materials that will assist them better in making the transition; this guide (*i*) would be ideal. After providing them with the tools, step back and observe what they do with them from a distance.

It is very rare that someone who is used to being "safe" will jump to an unsafe setting and bask in it. Trying to convince them to do so is like them trying to convince us to be like everyone else and join Corporate America. Do not look to convince! Provide the information and personal experiences of being an entrepreneur and let them make the choice if they would like to cross over or remain "everybody else."

You've made the decision to spend a few years of your life in ways most people wouldn't, so that you can spend the rest of your life like others can't.

Create. Work smart. Be the master of your destiny. Accept the greatness in which you are and mind your damn business!

20

Enjoy the Process

---

*That can be anything
from waiting for deals
or decisions from
counterparts or
negatives that come
with the life.*

Take the amazing with the unbearable
and embrace it! There will be more times
than many that you will want to quit, and
on certain days, you actually will quit!

Once you return (because you will, rather
quickly), you need to have something to
remind you of your "why." Your "why" is

your reason for starting a company to provide a particular service. Your "why" is also what you store in your private thoughts or daydream about working out. You know, making the *Forbes* list, or getting more girls, or doing the *Tonight Show*. Your "why" will drive you and will greatly assist you in enjoying the process of entrepreneurship.

Over time, you will learn to enjoy the process of what it is to create your brand, build your brand, and maintain your brand.

Like anything else in life, it takes time, patience, and growth to get to the point of enjoying the process. That process can be anything from waiting for deals or decisions from counterparts or negatives that come with the life. The feeling of successfully obtaining or finishing a deal should NOT be the ONLY time you have a sense of enjoyment as an entrepreneur.

It's been said before about entrepreneurship being a roller-coaster ride. On a roller coaster, you enjoy the buildup to the top and you brace yourself to enjoy the plunge to the bottom! You enjoy both processes and the different thrill each brings. It's scary as hell and has a lot of twists and turns but it's so worth it!

Do NOT get down on yourself for making mistakes; you won't always be right. Also, don't get high off yourself for making major moves; treat everything like it's your first project. In the words of Derrick James, "Be on the humble, yo." In the beginning it's easier said than done. Stick around for a while: It becomes easier done than said.

Conclusion

Although your journey will be different, these principles will take you very far on the road to becoming a successful entrepreneur. Enjoy your journey like i hope you enjoyed this guide! Don't rush through the pathway to your ultimate goal. Life is about who makes it, not about who makes it the fastest. People eventually want to know your story, whether you make millions of dollars or not. You are making a difference and you are doing it in an unconventional way ... YOUR way!

It takes a huge set of *cojones* and a great deal of self-confidence to take the leap as an entrepreneur. The smartest thing you can ever do as an entrepreneur is, "Never give up."

You will endure times when you hit rock bottom and it looks as if there is no way to the top. The key word is "looks." As we know, "looks" are deceiving and a true entrepreneur "sees" a way up from the bottom. These segment titles alone can direct your path on your journey.

If need be, forget these explanations and fill in your own from the titles. i can guarantee that you will experience, exercise, or endure every single segment title that makes up this guide.

Go be great and enjoy your journey. Remember, the most important word in entrepreneurship is....

(Hint: It's the title of the damn book!)

Afterword

i intentionally refrained from telling MY story in this guide. Although the segments are things i've been through, i wanted to keep it strictly about things young entrepreneurs will go through or need to know.

i am what i like to call an "occasional skim reader," so when thinking about writing this book, i wanted everything to be exactly how i am.

i wanted to write every single word and structure every sentence. i am very professional but i am also a black kid from the inner city of Dallas, so this book wouldn't be me without a little bit of slang.

i also wanted the segments to be brief and to the point. i usually skim-read on planes, heading to meetings or boxing matches. i sometimes re-read the same book or chapters for the inspiration.

i

What i find to be really cool about this book (if i can say so myself) is that it was written across four countries. i began writing it in Montreal, Canada, then continued to poke at it while in the United States. A short time later, i took my thoughts to San Juan, Puerto Rico, and finished the book in Melbourne, Australia. Everything was spread out across six months, but i got it done.

You can go sit down with another entrepreneur and i'm sure they can give you 20 pointers on what to look out for or how to make different adjustments along your journey. i have to stress, this is my mind and my thoughts at 29 years old, six years into being my own boss. i'm more than sure by my 10th year, at age 33, i'll be able to write another guide for entrepreneurs; that one will be on another level, and with another mindset.

My hope is that young entrepreneurs and/or aspiring entrepreneurs find themselves and their passions while reading *i*. i also hope that those who lack

the knowledge or need the guidance
entering entrepreneurship will pick up
this book and finish it with a strongly
motivated spirit in preparation for their
journey.

Adrian "AC" Clark founded AC Sports Management, LLC, in 2012. A native of Dallas, Texas, Clark began representing professional athletes in 2010 at the age of 24, shortly after graduating from Texas A&M University-Corpus Christi with a B.A. in Communications (PR/Media).

At age 25, Clark was certified by the National Basketball Players Association as a Player Agent. Clark is also a licensed Boxing Manager and has negotiated more than $500,000 in purses for his clients.

In 2016, *Forbes* named Clark to its annual "30 Under 30" list of the brightest young entrepreneurs, breakout talents and change agents.

2016

Made in the USA
Coppell, TX
24 June 2021

58014283R00066